Sonder

THOUGHT PROVOKING POETRY & PROSE

D.G. TORRENS

Copyright © 2020 D.G. Torrens
SONDER
Edition 1.

This is a work of fiction. Names, characters, businesses, places, events, and incidents either are the products of the author's imagination or used in a fictitious manner. Any resemblance to actual persons, living or dead, or actual events is purely coincidental.

License Notes: This eBook/paperback is licensed for your personal enjoyment only. This eBook may not be re-sold or given away to other people. If you would like to share this eBook with another person, please purchase an additional copy for each person you share it with.

If you are reading this eBook and did not purchase it, or it was not purchased for your use only, then you should return to Amazon.com and purchase your own copy. Thank you for respecting the hard work of this author.

All rights reserved. No part of this eBook may be reproduced, stored in a retrieval system, or transmitted in any form or by any means without the prior written permission of the author

Publisher D.G. Torrens
ISBN: 9781096013693

All images used in this publication sourced CCO from Pixabay.com free for public domain use.

Author's Note

Poetry is a unique and personal voice delivered by the author to encourage the reader to feel from deep within. Sonder delivers poetry that also explores the lives of others through the author's metaphorical lens.

Sonder – *Everyone has a story*

The realisation that each random passer-by is living a life as vivid and complex as your own—populated with their own ambitions, friends, routines, worries and inherited craziness—an epic story that continues invisibly around you like an anthill sprawling deep underground, with elaborate passageways to thousands of other lives that you'll never know existed, in which you might appear only once, as an extra sipping coffee in the background, as a blur of traffic passing on the highway, as a lighted window at dusk.

— *JOHN KOENIG -THE DICTIONARY OF OBSCURE SORROWS*

Not everyone will understand your journey

What matters is that you do –

— D.G. TORRENS

Sunset to Sunrise

She observed thousands of sunsets
And always rose with the sun
Her tired feet journeyed for miles
But now she was spent and done

Her hands bore witness to her struggles
But never once did she complain
She would go down with the sunset
And rise with the sun again

Her children passed before her
Too weak to fight the fight
Her broken heart remained broken
She lost her inner sight

The dry terrain and empty wells
Finally brought her to her knees
A smile escaped and reached her eyes
Throw my ashes into the breeze

For my children they await me
No need for you to grieve
My journey was an arduous one
Now I must take my leave.

In the Face of Strangers

I took a seat by the window
In a busy coffee shop
I leaned back in my chair
And sipped my coffee
Passers-by caught my attention
I observed their faces and wondered
Are their lives as complex as mine?
Do they submerge into their emotions –
And struggle with their day?
My answers swam in the tears
Falling from a woman's eyes
She struggled through the crowds
Navigating a wheelchair
I LOOKED ON CLOSER
A young child smiled at me from her wheelchair
I smiled back
Her lower limbs were missing
AND YET SHE SMILED
In that moment - all my troubles faded away.

Body Beautiful

You served me well
When I was weak
When I poisoned my body
When I broke me

You served me well
When I fought against you
Repairing me without question
When I was through

You served me well
You never let me down
You gave me the strength
So, I would not drown

You served me well
You kept me standing
When I should have fallen
You were so outstanding

You fought the great fight
When it was me against me
My body beautiful
I will never doubt thee.

Echo Chamber

I found myself in an echo chamber
Filled with interests self-served
My views and thoughts were drowning
Least of all could not be heard

A room immersed in white noise
Judgemental lips moving
I stand tall and poised
I know they're disapproving

With no knowledge gained
I swiftly take my leave
I hear the people whisper
They don't affect me

If there is no debate
Very little is achieved
It's never too late
In this I believe

A collective wisdom
A measure of words
From all sides is needed
For a world without swords.

Siblings in State Care

Tired and worn I pack my bag
Where am I going?
What children's home next
Social services were busy
With their safety checks
Tired and worn I pack my bag
Torn from our home
With my siblings in tow
I encourage them forward
For them - strength I show
Tired and worn I pack my bag
I wipe their tears
From their sodden face
Hold their hands
Until we reach our new place
Tired and worn I pack my bag
Constantly on the move
From home to home
Feeling unloved
And totally alone
Tired and worn I pack my bag
A child needs security
And parents that care
Not the uncertainty
They are forced to bear
Tired and worn I pack my bag
Rarely the same bed
No time to make friends
We cling to each other
My sisters and brother.

(For my siblings and me)

Our true self is revealed

When our emotions are elevated

— *D.G. TORRENS*

Beneath an Indian Sunset

Beneath an Indian sunset
While the chulla burns
She warms her weary body
As the paratha turns

Corn stalks ignite the flames
While tears trail down her cheeks
Time is running out
She leaves in less than a week

Invisible tears rain on her heart
While her eyes rest on the corn pile
But deep inside she is breaking
And forcing an outward smile.

She Views the World

She views the world
With a wisdom bestowed
From a life journeyed
Through tears she's owed

She views the world
With sadness in her heart
As it crumbles before her
While the skies turn dark

She views the world
With tears in her eyes
For what has been lost
For what has died

She observes the destruction
Brought on by human greed
The people carry on regardless
As war and famine increase.

Only the Genuine

She came to realise
People cannot be trusted
Let down too often
A new life she constructed
With not too many people
Just a chosen few
Ones she can rely on
Who will see her through
When at death's door
Only genuine hearts
She wants by her bedside
When she departs
The years have brought her wisdom
Her candor is well known
It took an entire lifetime
For her life to be her own.

I Found Me

I found happiness in places
I once took for granted
I sought peace within me
Where once there was war
I found love in my child
where my own mother did not
I battled my struggles
And turned them into journeys
I discovered acceptance
In a life I once rejected
I journeyed my life
Full of tests and trials
And with all the wisdom gained
I finally found me.

Chasing Shadows

I am chasing shadows
That cannot be caught
It took me sometime
With efforts I wrought

My answers were embedded
Far beneath my corium
Where my true self struggled
To stay out the crematorium

I searched deep and hard
A moment of clarity reveals
All humans are floored
And hide behind shields

Some people feel deeper
Thus, battle with their heart
A beautiful trait
That sets them apart

So, chasing shadows
That cannot be caught
Was not totally fruitless
A battle I fought.

Firefly

Like the firefly
I shine at night
Wielding my words
As my soul ignites

Darkness is divergent
Where miracles occur
I write through the night
The dark is my lure

My written words lead me
To truth and light
Like the resplendent firefly
That radiates the night

Charged with hope
My fingers dance
Across the keyboard
Like a true romance

All my worries fade away
While my internal light glows
Guiding me through the night
Inspiring my creative prose

Like the firefly
I shine at night
Wielding my words
As my soul ignites.

Sometimes you must tread

Rough terrain

Before your feet can journey

A smooth road –

— *D.G. TORRENS*

Streets of Delhi

Dusk settles on the streets of Delhi
Street vendors shouting by my jalebi
A wandering cow grinds me to a halt
The rickshaw swerves, drivers not at fault
A smile emerges on my face
As the cow is moved to clear the space
A city alive fills me with wonder
As I am pulled to the side, no time to ponder
My eyes rest upon a homeless dog
A regular sight amidst the Delhi smog
Wagging his tail eyes wide open
I kneel down, his spirit unbroken
I stroke his face and open my hand
He inches closer proud and grand
The streets of Delhi filled with dreams
Never-ending traffic with horns that scream
Alight with spirit alive with pride
My Delhi love, I carry with pride.

Faith in Love Restored

He noticed her in the background
Disconnected from the crowd
Her smile reached inside of him
Unspoken words so loud

He found his feet moving
His eyes locked with hers
He knew his heart was taken
His faith in love restored.

Measuring You

I will measure you
By your deeds
And not by your colour
And not by your creed
I will not measure you
By your bank balance
Not by your car
And not by your talent
I will measure you
By your treatment of animals
Not by your success
Not by your valuables
The true measure of a person
Is summed up to me
By how they treat others
And how they treat me.

Mother Earth's Warning

This planet is my gift
That no human owns
It's not yours to split
It's everyone's home
A new world emerges
People forced to adjust
Mother earth urges
Humanity – I cannot trust
The smog has disappeared
The buildings can be seen
Like in the beginning
A beautiful dream
Rivers run clear
And the air is renewed
But for how long
If the humans pursue
Mother earth cries,
You forced my hand
I need to make changes
To save my land
I need to act now
Before my planet dies
I know this is hard
I can hear your cries
You must hear me now
Before it's too late
Replenish I vow
Be patient and wait
Please understand you are renting space
On my once fruitful land
You treated with disgrace

I beg you all – don't force my hand
You arrive with nothing
And leave much the same
You need to change your thinking
Before I go up in flames.

2020 The Virus – Earth's Vaccine

An Eventual return
To normality is craved
But a new norm is needed
For our world to be saved

A return to normality
With polluted air
Surely, we've learned something
Unless nobody cares

Waters run clear
The fish can be seen
The lands are recovering
The virus – earth's vaccine

Against human destruction
Mother earth had no choice
We had to be stopped
She has forced her voice

I hear you now
I cannot speak for the masses
A new norm is needed
Before the earth turns to ashes

An eventual return
To normality is craved
But a new norm is needed
For our planet to be saved.

2020 –
(The year our world stood still)

Focus on where you finish

And not where you started

Your beginnings do not

Define your end –

— *D.G. TORRENS*

Mother Nature's Unwanted Gift

Mother Nature bestows me a gift
I am a woman now
But I am not ready
Where was my childhood? Something I missed
Mother Nature remains silent
While my body bleeds
But I am not ready
Where was my childhood? Something I missed
I glare at my reflection
And all is changed
Mother Nature remains silent
My memories cry down my cheeks
While my finger sweeps my scars
I am not ready
Where was my childhood? Something I missed
I am still a child
Until I've been a child
Take back your gift
For I am not ready
Where was my childhood? Something I missed.

Hush

My skin burns with pain
Yet I remain silent
All dignity removed
HUSH
Be quiet little girl
My skin burns – I feel no more pain
NUMB
My spirit broken
WHY
What did I do wrong today?
HUSH
Be quiet little girl
CLICK
Locks the bolt on my bedroom door
HUSH
Be quiet little girl
I awake from my slumber –
Half dreaming
My breathing laboured
Oh, mummy what did I do wrong today?
HUSH
In that moment –
My nightmare revealed
It's ok
You are a child no more.

Her Mind Tranquil

She reclines in her chair
Filled with pride
For all her accomplishments
Fought against the tide
She raises her brow
Lips curl into a smile
Her journey complete
Though it took a while
Her arm extends
Reaching for her glass
She sips slowly
While the seconds pass
Savouring the moment
While all is still
Filled with peace
Her mind tranquil.

We All Make Mistakes

We all make mistakes
My laundry list is long
But I've learned from them all
And it's made me strong

I've taken the road less travelled
Avoiding all the signs
I've taken many risks
And crossed numerous lines

But I am only human
Not a perfect sphere
I do not regret a thing
Even the times I feared.

A Journey for Answers

I forage for answers that allude me
My questions are many
My curiosity aplenty
I journeyed through mountains
Much wisdom I gained
Much strength I attained
I battled through rivers barely afloat
The current was strong
The passage long
Much fear I felt – but I was alive
Thriving on the unknown
Thriving on my own
As my arduous journey neared its end
I knew who I was
I finally knew me –

Sometimes, silence is

The most powerful weapon–

— *D.G. TORRENS*

Luminescent Moon

The luminescent moon casts its glow
Radiating the world out of darkness below
Illuminated trees dance under its guide
While the vast oceans bring in the tide
After dark streets come alive with music
Like singers on stage performing their acoustics
After skulking in the shadows during the day
The wildlife emerges to assail their prey
As the sun rises and the moon goes to sleep
All goes quiet for night-time to keep
When the luminescent moon will again glow
Radiating the world out of darkness below.

Captain Tom Moore

Captain Tom Moore
A beacon of hope
You brought tears to my eyes
And a lump to my throat
A hero of our time
For which we are grateful
A fly past in your honour
For a soldier so respectful
One hundred today
Thirty million raised
The world is clapping
You deserve this praise
Captain Tom Moore
You have raised our spirits
Shown us what's possible
We should silence for a minute
For all those complaining
Breaking lockdown rules
This is what a hero looks like
Captain Tom Moore - a British jewel
Happy Birthday brave soldier
For your selfless efforts once more

An incredible human being
This world needed – Captain Tom Moore.

*For Tom
(2020 Lockdown)* –

Two Solitary Beings

Her face pressed against the window
Alone in her shabby flat
She watches the raindrops tumbling
While stroking her aging cat

Her parents long ago passed
No siblings – and cousins are none
Her solitude deliberately chosen
After those that she loved had gone

No wish to make friends
To transient for her
Alone with her cat
She smiles as he purrs

Two solitary beings
Living side by side
Their chosen path
By which they are tied.

Under a Starless Sky

Under a Starless Sky
I navigate the streets
Avoiding the cracks
Beneath my feet
The fog descends
Clouding my view
I continue forward
Straight into you
With your guiding hand
You navigate the way
Out of the darkness
Away from today –

Beautiful Girl

He looks to the sky
And smiles at the blue
The birds are ascending
And the sun is out to

He ambles ahead
And she catches his eye
The beautiful girl
As she passes by

He stops in his tracks
Looking over his shoulder
She offers him a smile
He begins to smoulder

She takes the initiative
And offers her number
He's elated inside
But contains his rumba

She turns on her heels
Walking away
The beautiful girl
He met today

He looks to the sky
Fist-punches the air
Today was a good day
Nothing can compare.

Deceived

You conned your way to my heart
Then mercilessly tore it to shreds
You placed me on a pedestal
To watch me fall apart
You cast your net
You reeled me in
Like a lamb to the slaughter
Shredding my skin
You hung me out to dry
Then walked away
Closing your ears
To my desperate cry –

Onset Agoraphobia

Too scared to leave her house
A place of safety
A place she trusts
While the world is spinning into dust
The economy is collapsing
There is civil unrest
She's safe at home in her security nest
But nothing is certain
Except for today
The news is grim no hope on the way
People are jobless
Families going hungry
2020 is feared by every country
Covid 19
Bubonic plague
Even Ebola doing the rounds but vague
She's scared to leave her house
A place of safety
A place she trusts
For her sanity – her routine is a must.

2020 –
(The year our world stood still)

Wings are for flying

Not cages

So, spread your wings

And fly like an eagle –

— *D.G. TORRENS*

No Words

Her feelings leak from her eyes
Her unmoving lips part silently
But he hears her unspoken words
Her message was delivered
Straight to his heart.

Choose Your Battles Wisely

You invited me to your battleground
I accepted
I corrected my stance
And fought you with words
You could not handle
My choice of weaponry
So you conceded
My words were my shield
And brought you to your senses
- Choose your battles wisely –

Memories

Memories trail down her face
Like rain on a bleak winter's day
Tears of sorrow
For a time since passed
When life consumed her
And all that she was
Memories trail down her face
Like rain on a bleak winter's day
Tears of longing
For all that is lost
Memories are all that's left
Trailing down her face
Soaked up in her tears
For a time since passed.

A Murder of Crows

A murder of crows
perched on a tree
Loud and rambunctious
People fear thee
Urban legends
Sweep our minds
But social and caring
You will find
A murder of crows
Perched in a tree
Should not be feared
As per history
Wise and clever
Surveying their space
Picking you out
They'll recognise your face
A murder of crows
Are not a threat
A murder of dictators
Now that I would bet
When did you hear?
That crows did kill.
A story I'm guessing
Told to chill –

Secret Feelings

Secret feelings
You are not hers
Yet you are all she thinks about
Secret feelings
You emerge in her dreams
Wanting her as she wants you
Secret feelings
A desire so strong
She can hardly breathe –
Secret feelings
She needs to see you just once
To feel your lips on hers
Secret feelings –

Not Just a Dream

I submerge into dream state
Gone for a while
Deeper and deeper I descend
Until I find me
Lost in dense woods
The whispers of the night
Draw my attention
While the cool night
Brushes my shoulders
Dry leaves crunch beneath my feet
The slightest sound
Magnifies my fears
My heart races
My breaths quicken
I pick up my pace
While my eyes dart all around
I trip and fall into a bottomless pit
There is nothing to break my fall
THIS IS IT – MY END IS NIGH
I reconcile with my unfortunate end
Because in this moment I realise –
The footprints I leave behind
- Are worth following -
And when I awaken
My lips curl into a smile.

Spectators will judge and point fingers

Loved ones will extend their hand

— *D.G. TORRENS*

The Truth Deepens the Pain

When you need someone the most
You often hear their footsteps
Fade into the distance
The ones who say they have your back
Are often the ones
Responsible for breaking it
And the truth of this
Deepens the pain
But our knowledge is enriched
Becoming our armour
Against future falls.

Thoughts Unrevealed

Alone with her thoughts
Unrevealed and unprotected
Thoughts she cannot share
For the aftershock she fears
Alone with her thoughts
Erupting inside of her
Tearing her apart
Breaking her down little by little
Alone with her thoughts
Fighting their urge to break free
To be released from the tortuous pain
Self-inflicted and all-consuming
Alone with her thoughts.

Understanding the Wise Old Owl

I understand now
'The wise old owl'
Knowledge gained throughout our life's journey
There are no shortcuts
Just experience
And complete understanding
You must partake in life
And all its ups and downs
To gain the knowledge of
'The wise old owl'.

All I Need I Have

My eyes adjust to the light
Streaming through the blinds
I feel the sun brush against my skin
Raising a smile on my face
I see the beauty in my day
Supplied by Mother Nature
And in this sublime moment
Mother Nature reveals –
All I need, I have.

The Magpie and Me

One for sorrow
The saying goes
Tip your hat
Old wives scream out
I lock my eyes
With the magpie before me
Instead –
I embrace this daily routine
With the magpie
Who resides in my tree
Staring me out
Protecting his ground
While his babies cry out
From inside my tree
I smile then slowly turn away
Walking towards my door
Bad luck – this magpie
Will never bestow me
For he knowingly
Lives safely in my tree.

There for Her

She felt the warmth of your kindness
She heard the concern in your voice
She reached for your extended hand
Amidst the chaotic noise

Like an angel you appeared
At a low point in her life
When she was all alone
Surrounded by trouble and strife –

I See a Door

I see a door
It is wide open
I step closer
And peek in
An empty room greets me –
Nothing but bare walls
Confused
I step closer
I look on with new sight
I see a room
Bright
Filled with life
Welcoming me in
I smile
It's not just an empty room
It is potential
I just needed to open my eyes.

I believe in infinite possibility

I believe in me –

— *D.G. TORRENS*

Moving Lips

My eyes cruised the room
Filled with discontent
All the lips were moving
But not a word was meant

Eyebrows raise and lips curl
White noise spread so fast
I took my leave without a thought
Relieved to be gone at last.

Pain is most severe

When delivered by those you trust –

— D.G. TORRENS

Distorted Image

We go to great lengths
To starve our curves
Resculpting our bodies
That we should preserve

There is nothing more beautiful
Than our God given shell
I just want to scream
But my cries I quell

Airbrushed imperfections
Filters of every kind
Sought by perfection seekers
Impelled to be blind

We should where our skin
Like a badge of honour
Each mark we acquire
Should make us stronger

Our body is but a vessel
For our goods to keep
We need to be awakened
From this clouded sleep.

Remove Your Shield

I recognised in you
A shield of sorts
You notice me staring
And turn away
I know that smile
Delivered to the world
The one that says
I'm fine go away
But I see in you
What's deep in me
A guard so strong
Like mine I see
I see you –
I smile
Your shield does not work with me
As mine does not work with you
I see in you –
What is deep in me
A maze of emotions
A labyrinth of pain
I see your battle
And no not its name
You see my battle

And no not its name
I lower my shield and extend my hand
I reveal –
'Hi, my name is depression'
You take my hand and reply
'Hi, my name is grief'
I see you now and you see me
Sometimes, our shields cannot save us
Sometimes, we need to remove them
To be saved –

Heart Whispers

My heart whispers your name
Awakening me from my slumber
I place my hand over my heart
Each beat reinforcing my feelings
Reminding me that love never fades
Your name echoes through my body
Igniting a tsunami of emotions
Tearing through my veins
I gasp –
For my heart has conveyed a message
You will always own my heart.

My Heart Belongs to Me

I am battle ready
A fortress I have built
My armour impenetrable
No longer weak
For you made me strong
When you slain my heart
Seared by the shards
I piece me together
And my scars serve as a reminder
My heart belongs to me.

If you can think it

You can do it

Possibility is infinite –

— *D.G. TORRENS*

I See You

You gifted me your vulnerability
The purest part of you
Revealing all that you are
I am intoxicated by your truths
My heart overwhelmed
There is sublime beauty in your candor
Displayed before me like a Picasso
I no longer look on with confusion
For I see you now with great clarity.

Behind the Smile

You have taken up space
In the corner of my mind
A welcome guest
That encourages my smile
I close my eyes to see you
To visualise you close to me
I can almost touch you
You envelope me with your arms
- THERE YOU ARE –
Behind my closed eyes
Behind my smile
That raises other's curiosity
You are my one private thing
The one behind my smile –

Secret Desire

She wants to feel your breath
Whispering to her neck
The touch of your hands
Upon her body
Your fingers laced through hers
But for now
She must wait
-Until time allows-

Turn off the Volume

A plethora of words spills from your lips
A crime to my ears
I switch off the sound and my thoughts trail off
My eyes dart to meet your lips
Still your mouth is moving
Unaware that you lost me
I watch a robin and tune into its song
Music to my ears
The corners of my mouth turn up
I conclude
Some people don't deserve the gift of speech.

Merging Hearts

My lips curl into a smile
My chest rises and falls with rapid breaths
You rake your fingers through your hair
While inching closer to me
You extend your hand
I lace my fingers through yours
You press your lips to mine
I feel your chest pounding
And in this sublime moment
I know your heart is mine –

Brought Back to Life

I languish in your words
Seeping through my soul
Igniting my every emotion
You brought me back to life
For I was dead
No longer wandering aimlessly
Through the midst of life
Your words reach deep into my soul
Awakened me from a deep sleep
I hear them
I feel them
Like divine intervention
You brought me back to life –

They say absence makes

The heart grow fonder

But absence also makes

The heart grow smarter –

— D.G. TORRENS

Assassin With a Smile

They will feast and pillage
On our weaknesses
Assassins with smiles
Pleasuring in our falls
Drinking in our failures
Like vintage champagne
Something to savour
While our tears descend
And our heart cries beats of pain
Assassins with smiles
They can revel in my pain
For my tears are real
And convey all that I am.

Memories and Time

The chambers of my mind
A complex labyrinth of images
Collected over time
My memories ascend
Tears rain down my face
A reminder there is no end
Time does not allow you to forget
Time is ever constant
Carrying our memories
Even those we regret.

Awakened

My soul awakened from a deep sleep
For years, my empty heart did weep
My focus on my physical being
Neglecting my soul that needed freeing
No longer feeling like something is missing
I know who I am no longer drifting.

Chaotic Mind

I am wandering through the tunnels of my mind
Chaos has unfolded
I navigate my frustration
Push aside my anxiety
Run through my confusion
And there I find me
Dazed and lost
I take me by the hand
Silence descends
Chaos now quietened
I lead me through the calm
The chaos is no more.

My tears are all the words

I cannot share –

— D.G. TORRENS

The River Inside

A raging river flows within me
Its current is rapid and strong
I am an unwilling passenger
As it pulls me along

I change my perception
And my fears are released
I flow with the river
My strength now increased.

For My Child it Will be Different

I look to my own child
With love I have showered
With my promises fulfilled
She is strong and empowered

My greatest masterpiece
She's happy and flourishing
Has never known pain
Only a mother's nurturing

I gave her the childhood
I dreamed of for myself
She will grow up treasuring memories
To me, the greatest form of wealth.

For Lilliah x

I Matured With Pain

I matured with pain
And buckets of tears
With each step taken
Over the years
My tears are memories
You cannot see
Trailing my cheeks
Knowing nothing is free
The pain I carry
Deep in my heart
Was delivered to me
From the very start
My trauma responses
Remind me each day
The neglect of a child
Never goes away.

Real Treasure

We seek our trinkets
And material treasures
That fades and corrodes
You will find
Not realising our real treasure
Stands the test of time.

Ageing

Ageing will follow us it cannot be stopped
But our attitudes towards it can be dropped
It's just a number – we should all be proud
We have made it this far so shout it out loud
Don't be afraid no need to fear
There will always be those who look on and sneer
These ones my friend are not worth your time
Age will catch up with them soon they will find
Think of the children you've loved and raised
One day they'll thank you your life will be praised
The knowledge you've passed down over the years
Is now their guide to overcome fears
So, look in the mirror and smile wide
Don't be afraid and sit inside
Your life is not over there is much to do
Now grab those reins and think of you.

Snowy England

A single flake floating down
I watch it fall making not a sound
The heavens open wide and fast
Illuminating trees and the sky so vast
I stand frozen while it falls
Upon my head and body all
Looking ahead to the fallen snow
Smiling now because I know
Little England is standing still
For just a moment – our land tranquil.

Words are Wisdom

I quell my voice
For nothing can be gained
The ignorant don't hear
They only complain
I won't waste my words
When they can be best served
On interested ears
That want to observe
When wisdom is shared
We gain and grow
The knowledge we devour
From words bestowed
It expands our world
Opens doors that were shut
Giving us advantages
We otherwise disrupt
Words are powerful
More so than weapons
A far greater tool
Than any snake's venom
Words prevent wars
Bring peace and prevent conflict
Sadly, the powerful ignorant
Prefer we run the gauntlet
The world is in decline
Yet it could be fixed
But fixing loses money
So, we are stuck with this
I shall quell my voice
For nothing is gained
When words fall on deaf ears
My tears fall like rain.

Walking blindly the signs

Allude us

While an imminent storm is circling –

— *D.G. TORRENS*

Mother Earth Cries

Mother earth cries
I need a break
Please stop
So, I can replenish my once plentiful world
I need to clean the air
Clean the waters
And cool down
Mother earth cries
I need a break
I won't last long if you persist
I am dying and I need your help
I cannot do this alone
Mother earth cries
I need a break
Adhere my warning before it's too late
In the beginning, I gave you everything
A bountiful world with all that you needed
Led by greed, you have taken too much
Soon there will be nothing left
Mother earth cries
I need your help
I cannot do this alone
If you keep doing what you are doing
I am going to die
And there will be nothing left –

For You – My World is Closed

All my doors are closed to you now
The door to my heart
The door to my mind
And the door to my world
There is no door left for you to break down –

We are living in cages

Of our own design

You must change your thinking

To open the cage –

— *D.G. TORRENS*

Solitary Moment

Finding a solitary moment
Amidst the chaos of life
To drown out white noise
That clutters my mind
Irritating words
Like pollen in the air
A crime to my ears
I need to escape –
William Blake, Shakespeare, and Wordsworth I crave
To replace the insult
On words today
The beauty of our language
Decimated by many parting lips –

Lifting You Out of Darkness

For so long I believed it was me
Apologising constantly to satisfy thee
Living with your darkness
You played on my weakness
Breaking me down
Until I drowned
For so long, I believed it was me
Your lack of emotion ignoring my plea
Confused daily, I questioned myself
Ignored and forgotten left on the shelf
Your constant dark mood filled me with dread
There were so many times, I wished I were dead
But I found the strength to understand
That you were broken and needed a hand
Instead of leaving, I extended my love
To heal you slowly and not dispose of
The easiest thing was to walk away
But I knew I could show you a better way –

Depression

Depression feels like
A tranquil river that flows
Then without warning –
A raging storm emerges
Breaking the riverbanks
Creating chaos all around
UNTIL –
Once again, a tranquil river flows.

I Miss You

I miss you
Every single day
I long for your arms to envelope me
To feel your breath whispering to my neck
I miss you
Every single day
The way your smile reaches your eyes –
On sight of me
I miss you
Every single day
My heart is in mourning
For what can never be
I miss you –

Doing the right thing

Is not always the popular choice

But doing nothing – is worse

— *D.G. TORRENS*

Everything is Changing

Everything is changing
Nothing is certain
The world I once knew
Now behind a veiled curtain

Proximities now reduced
People afraid to touch
Hugging feels like a crime
Yet, we need one so much

Enveloped in fear
People tread with caution
Our safety nets gone
Nothing is certain –

2020 – (The year our world stood still)

Wounded Soldier

A wounded soldier on the ground
The sound of gunfire all around
A fleeting thought passes through his mind
As all his comrades are far behind

No one is winning – only death
To collect the ones who have breathed their last breath
This moment of clarity he understands
When he reaches out with an extended hand

To the soldier beside him who has been taken
By death waiting he was not mistaken
He closed his eyes accepting his fate
Praying to God to open his gate.

A Reminder

The warmth of the sun discarded
Replaced by an angry storm
The birds take cover in hiding
While mother nature performs

Reminding us this is her world
The wind ravishes the land
Putting us in our place
Mother nature makes her stand.

Life as we Know It

Life as we know it has gone forever
Our climate is changing and not for the better
The ice caps are melting, and the oceans are growing
This happened so quickly without us knowing
The seasons we relied upon are not as they were
Traditional summers are now just a blur
There are so many reasons this could have happened
Finally, now we are all awakened
Could it be a question of too little too late?
And this is to be our imminent fate
Or can we turn this world around
Keep the oceans at bay and our feet on the ground.

No Regrets

I do not regret my words
For they spilled from my heart's reserves
My feelings I had to impart
I confess from the very start
So, know my heart chose you
With the deepest of love so true –

We are often guided

through our toughest times

By the unexpected –

— *D.G. TORRENS*

Thoughts Unrevealed

Alone with my thoughts
Unrevealed and unprotected
Thoughts I cannot share
For the aftershocks I fear
Alone with my thoughts
Erupting inside of me
Tearing me apart
Breaking me down little by little
Alone with my thoughts
Fighting their urge to break free
To be released from this tortuous pain
Self-inflicted and all-consuming
Alone with my thoughts.

Dying Planet

Where once a river flowed
Now lies an empty bed
Where once a forest bloomed
Now concrete jungles root
Where once the fields were sewn
Now derelict farms stand
Where once the sky was clear
Now smog pollutes the air
When summers were summers
And winters were winters
The seasons have taken leave
We are left with a world so broken
Now impossible to repair
Our world once plentiful
That catered all our needs
Our planet now crying
The tears are displayed
in its total devastation –
But it's never too late
We can change course
Where once a river flowed.

Confused and Dazed

Confused and dazed
Decisions made in haste
White noise deafening
My feet running
I want to scream
For I am locked in a dream
Panicked and scared
My thoughts unshared
I want to exit right
But my heart diverts me left
I am deeply bereft
Confused and dazed
Decisions made in haste –

Kindness does not seek an audience

Just a recipient in need of help –

Is all the audience that's needed

Don't be kind just to be seen

Be kind –

When unseen is the greatest act of unselfishness

True kindness can bestow

— *D.G. TORRENS*

The Whispers of the Land

The whispers of the land
Innocents beneath the ground
Lives cut short – their souls broken
Listen carefully the land has spoken

Desolate land and charred remains
No one's winning – no one gains
Broken hearts and broken minds
War is not the answer are people blind

Amputees, orphans, and childless mothers
Dead sons, uncles, husbands, and brothers
Are the ones who suffer in the end
Not the leaders, dictators to war they send.

Lifetime Journey

It is the lifetime journey we travel in our mind
That truly tests our strength
The battles we fought within ourselves
The goals we set
The obstacles we placed in our way
The words we should have shared
But chose not to
The foolish pride that lost us someone
Forgiveness of a wrong we refuse to accept
The one we loved who broke our spirit
The times we said no when it should have been yes
The lifetime journey we travel in our mind –
Is the hardest journey of all
Each step we take
Every decision we make
Inevitably determines our unknown fate –

Grey Area

I live in the grey area
Between black and white
Where real life unfolds
And things aren't always right

I live in the grey areas
Where not everything is explained
Where emotions run wild
And my heart is pained

Yet, I chose to remain enveloped in grey
Where not everything is black or white
Where people leave and go astray
Where black is grey and white's not right.

His Story

He stood out from the crowd
His focus on her
Willing her to turn around
She glanced around the room
Her eyes locked with his
She was drawn to the story
He told with his eyes
The silence he shared
With his unmoving lips
She captures it all
Desperate to know more
Patiently she waits
For his story to unfold.

Following the crowd will not always

Lead you to your destination

Sometimes, you need to break away

And change direction

To get where you want to be -

— *D.G. TORRENS*

Mother Earth Cries – This is My House

This is my house
And you are my guests
Don't force my hand
Don't encourage me to evict you
I gave you the freedom to live freely
What's mine is yours
But you must remember
No part of my planet is yours to claim
You can live on my land
You can grow your crops
But don't cut down my trees
Or you will cut my throat
Don't pollute my rivers
Or you will poison me
I gave you the freedom to live freely
Don't take advantage
What's mine is yours
Please don't be greedy
Earth is your home
Don't destroy it
Once it's gone – it's gone.

My failures bestowed me great wisdom

And my success benefited greatly –

— *D.G. TORRENS*

Lockdown 2020

I'm lockdown crazy
I'm worldometer obsessed
I'm bleeding ink
I'm writing undressed
I'm awake during the night
I'm stalking the fridge
I'm tiptoeing the halls
I'm anxious a smidge
I'm home-schooling in daylight
I'm mowing the lawns too
I'm cleaning everything possible
I'm just trying to get through
I'm my child's voice of reason
I'm my child's safe place
I'm staying home for everyone
I'm keeping my child safe
I'm my own voice of reason
I'm not in a grave
I'm home with my child
I'm alive and safe
I'm thankful for our NHS
I'm thankful for their light
I'm thankful they are fighting
I'm praying they survive the fight.

(2020 The year our world stood still)

Sometimes, silence is all the words

that are needed –

— *D.G. TORRENS*

Poor but Rich

She rests her weary body
Under the burning sun
Many years have past
With this life, she is done
She did not acquire riches
Or set the world on fire
She cleaned the houses of others
Someone, her children admired
Her time has come to an end
She has nothing but wisdom to bestow
For her children all gathered
They know that she must go
She looks to all her children
While patiently at death's door
A smile reaches her eyes
She had everything and more.

Grandma's Gatekeeper

Her beloved Grandma is dying
So little time left to share
She clutches her phone crying
While pacing the floor in despair

A race against time
to say goodbye
Grandma's gatekeeper
Is telling a lie

The bridge has collapsed
There's no way to cross
Time has run out
Her Grandma relapsed

The grandchildren mourn
And close friends gather
A private memorial
Brings them together

Grandma's gatekeeper
Committed a moral crime
Her maker will ensure justice
It's just a matter of time.

R.I.P
1926 – 2020

Wisdom Gained

I have learned many lessons
Navigated many roads
I have made huge mistakes
And lost self-control
Amidst this I found myself
And I know who I am
It took me fifty years
Of life lessons I crammed
I have received what I wished for
And wished that I had not
Be careful what you wish for
Once received it's your lot
I became a wife
A mother too
I lost many loved ones
But I fought my way through
My wisdom gained
I share with my child
To arm her well
When she leaves for the wild.

(For L.T.P)

The Beginning of the End

The world is too beautiful
For the human race
We have destroyed the planet
We are a total disgrace

Animals extinction
We are not far behind
We abused this world
We have all lived blind

Homes need care
Or they fall apart
We neglected the house
There is no fresh start

The lands are burning
Floods are plenty
The beginning of the end
Our world soon empty

Yet still we continue
To ignore the truth
We deserve to lose
Our once beautiful roof

There is no teaching
Those who won't listen
We are witnessing the end
Of God's perfect vision.

Spectator's Judge

Spectator's will Judge
Point fingers and nudge
Too scared to live
Not prepared to give
Observers on the ground
Making judgemental sounds
Through the lens of others
Their opinions smother
They wish they were brave
But in truth are enslaved
Too scared to live
Not prepared to give
Life passes them by
While we question why?

The fog always clears eventually

Enabling us to see clearly –

— *D.G. TORRENS*

Patience

It takes the patience of a hunting panther
The passion for something greater than yourself
The determination of a soldier ant
The will of a God
The desire likened to a first love
Years journeying an arduous road
UNTIL –
That moment
The moment you dreamed about
The moment you persevered for
Has finally arrived
Patience brings with it many rewards
There is a long view and a short view
What is your dream worth?
Mine is worth the patience to see it through.

Humankind – Our Worst Enemy

Our world no longer makes sense to me
Compassion alludes the masses
Our filter of kindness
Buried in a perpetual abyss
Cruel is ruling and many suffer
I sense an apocalyptic cloud –
Is ready to unleash its contents
Blinded and deafened
We step forward
Controlled by our own ignorance
The signs are clear
Yet we do not see
Still we step forward
Eyes wide shut
No accountability
Only irreversible destruction
Humankind – our worst enemy.

The path you are on right now is not permanent

If you don't like the journey

Change the route –

— D.G. TORRENS

About the Author

D.G. Torrens – is a UK/USA international bestselling Author/Poet from Birmingham UK. D.G. has written and published 19 books over the last 9 years and is currently penning book 20, Amnesia (due for release 2021) D.G. is represented in the USA by Hershman Rights Management (HRM Literary Agents).

A prolific writer with a deep passion for the written word, D.G. is also a founding member of AuthorcityUK and Bestsellingreads.com. D.G's books can be found on all Amazon sites worldwide.

D.G. Torrens 2020.